Home Maintenance Log For

Address:

_____

_____

Date of Purchase:

_____

DEDICATION

This book is dedicated to all the homeowners and DIY vacation rental property owners out there!

You are my inspiration in producing books and I'm excited to help in the planning of your yearly home maintenance around the world!

How to Use this Yearly Home Maintenance Checklist Notebook:

The purpose of this yearly home maintenance journal is to keep all your various DIY home fix ups and property management organized in one easy to find spot.

Here are some simple guidelines to follow so you can make the most of using this book:

1. The first "Systems Maintenance by Month" section is for you to write out monthly which systems to check whether its cleaning the pipes or caulking the showers/sinks.... so you can go back there to be reminded of your maintenance schedule once a year.

2. Most ideas are inspired by something we have seen. Use the "Repairman Contact Information" section to use as a reminder which repairman, company name, phone number you contacted as you needed that information.

3. And even more pages with the "Appliance Information" section is great for taking notes on date of purchase, appliance bought, purchased from, price paid, serial number..so to be reminded later of all important information.

4. The "Appliance Repair Log" section is for you to keep a visual reminder of each appliance serviced, date of service, repairman's name, contact info, cost and much more.

5. The "Monthly Maintenance Log" section is for you to checklist smoke detectors checks, change furnace filters, and space to fill in other tasks that are required to be checked out on a monthly basis.

6. The "Quarterly Maintenance Log" section is for you to write out the date of checking the basement or crawl space for leaks, cleaning the fridge, baseboards, check shower drain, with space for initials of person performing said duties...helpful information for remembering later on.

7. The "Yearly Maintenance Log" today is for you to write out important tasks such as smoke detector battery check, carbon monoxide check, cleaning the gutters, and space to add more tasks to the list....so you can be reminded later on.

8. Finally, so many "Blank Notes" sections so as to lay out your plan of keeping up with your own home or that of your rental properties and much more!

9. Whether you've just started with buying your own personal residence, or you are a rental property mogul...you will want to write down all your property maintenance projects in this notebook to look back on and remember the things you've done for each property.

Systems Maintenance By Month

JANUARY
Clean Pipes (Descale overnight)
Clean Showerheads and Taps
Clean and Recaulk Shower/Sinks
Clear Ice Dams In Gutters

FEBRUARY
Deep Clean Oven and Stovetop
Clean Washer
Clean Dyer and Check Vent
Clean Dishwasher & Check Filter

MARCH
Deep Spring Clean
Check Roof for Soft Spots
Check Sump Pump
Clean Gutters

Systems Maintenance By Month

APRIL
Spring Clean Kitchen
Vacuum HVAC Unit
Inspect Attic
Have AC Tuned

MAY
Check Exhaust Fans
Check Ceiling Fan Blades/Dust
Check Weather Stripping
Fix Rust Spots

JUNE
Clean Window Wells
Remove Dead Limbs From Trees
Touchup Paint
Remove Dead Plants From Flowerbeds

Systems Maintenance By Month

JULY
Clean/Stain Deck
Maintain Garage Door
Power Wash Concrete
Check Ductwork for Leaks

AUGUST
Clean Garbage Disposal
Clean Out Freezer
Clean Window Treatments
Change Air Filters

SEPTEMBER
Flush Water Heater
Furnace Tune-Up
Check Pantry for Expired Food
Check Carbon Monoxide Detectors

Systems Maintenance By Month

OCTOBER	
	Remove Exterior Hoses & Drain
	Vacuum & Clean Furnace
	Deep Clean Microwave
	Winterize AC

NOVEMBER	
	Vacuum Fridge Coils
	Deep Clean Fridge
	Clean Fridge Drain Pan
	Clean Circuit Breakers

DECEMBER	
	Test Electrical Outlets
	Run Water in Unused Rooms
	Inspect Fire Extinguishers
	Replace Smoke Detector Batteries

Repairman Contact Information

Company Name:_____

Phone Number:_____

Email:_____

Technician Name:_____

Company Name:_____

Phone Number:_____

Email:_____

Technician Name:_____

Company Name:_____

Phone Number:_____

Email:_____

Technician Name:_____

Company Name:_____

Phone Number:_____

Email:_____

Technician Name:_____

Repairman Contact Information

Company Name:_____
Phone Number:_____
Email:_____
Technician Name:_____

Company Name:_____
Phone Number:_____
Email:_____
Technician Name:_____

Company Name:_____
Phone Number:_____
Email:_____
Technician Name:_____

Company Name:_____
Phone Number:_____
Email:_____
Technician Name:_____

Repairman Contact Information

Company Name:_____

Phone Number:_____

Email:_____

Technician Name:_____

Company Name:_____

Phone Number:_____

Email:_____

Technician Name:_____

Company Name:_____

Phone Number:_____

Email:_____

Technician Name:_____

Company Name:_____

Phone Number:_____

Email:_____

Technician Name:_____

Home Warranty Information:

Company:_____

Premium Paid:_____

Contract Length:_____

Policy Number:_____

Customer Service Number:_____

Online Login User Name:_____

Online Login Password:_____

Appliances Covered:

	Refrigerator			Ice Maker
	Stove			Garbage Disposal
	Washer			Other
	Dryer			Other
	Dishwasher			Other
	Built-In Microwave			Other
	Trash Compactor			Other

Home Warranty Information (Continued):

Systems Covered:

	Air Conditioning
	Heating
	Electrical
	Door Bell
	Smoke Detectors
	Ceiling Fans
	Water Heater

	Central Vac.
	Septic Pump
	Well Pump
	Other
	Other
	Other
	Other

Usage Log:

Date	What Was Serviced	Problem	Service Technician

Home Warranty Information (Continued):

Date	What Was Serviced	Problem	Service Technician

Appliance Information

Date of Purchase	Appliance	Purchased From	Price	Serial Number	Warranty

Appliance Information

Date of Purchase	Appliance	Purchased From	Price	Serial Number	Warranty

Appliance Information

Date of Purchase	Appliance	Purchased From	Price	Serial Number	Warranty

Appliance Repair Log

Date of Service	Appliance	Repairman	Contact Info	Cost	Warranty

Appliance Repair Log

Date of Service	Appliance	Repairman	Contact Info	Cost	Warranty

Appliance Repair Log

Date of Service	Appliance	Repairman	Contact Info	Cost	Warranty

Monthly Maintenance Log

Date	Check Smoke Detectors	Change Furnace Filter	Other:	Other:	Performed By (Initials)

Monthly Maintenance Log

Date	Check Smoke Detectors	Change Furnace Filter	Other:	Other:	Performed By (Initials)

Monthly Maintenance Log

Date	Check Smoke Detectors	Change Furnace Filter	Other:	Other:	Performed By (Initials)

Quarterly Maintenance Log

Date	Check Basement/Crawl Space For Leaks	Clean Fridge	Clean Baseboards	Check Shower/Sink Drain Issues	Performed By (Initials)

Quarterly Maintenance Log

Date	Check Basement/Crawl Space For Leaks	Clean Fridge	Clean Baseboards	Check Shower/Sink Drain Issues	Performed By (Initials)

Quarterly Maintenance Log

Date	Check Basement/Crawl Space For Leaks	Clean Fridge	Clean Baseboards	Check Shower/Sink Drain Issues	Performed By (Initials)

Yearly Maintenance Log

Date	Smoke Detector Batteries	Carbon Monoxide Detector	Clean Gutters	Other:	Other:	Performed By (Initials)

Yearly Maintenance Log

Date	Smoke Detector Batteries	Carbon Monoxide Detector	Clean Gutters	Other:	Other:	Performed By (Initials)

Yearly Maintenance Log

Date	Smoke Detector Batteries	Carbon Monoxide Detector	Clean Gutters	Other:	Other:	Performed By (Initials)

Notes

Notes

Notes

Notes

Notes

Notes

Notes

Notes

Notes

Notes

Notes

Notes

Notes

Notes

Notes

Notes

Notes

Notes

Notes

Notes

Notes

Notes

Notes

Notes

Notes

Notes

Notes

Notes

Notes

Notes

Notes

Notes

Notes

Notes

Notes

Notes

Notes

Notes

Notes

Notes

Notes

Notes

Notes

Notes

Notes

Notes

Notes

Notes

Notes

Notes

Notes

Notes

Notes

Notes

Notes

Notes

Notes

Notes

Notes

Notes

Notes

Notes

Notes

Notes

Notes

Notes

Notes

Notes

Notes

Notes

Notes

Notes

Notes

Notes

Notes

Notes

Notes

Notes

Notes

Notes